Recorder Consorts

The music of Bach, Melchior Franck, Handel,
van Noordt, Pasquini, Philips & Quantz
arranged by Dom Gregory Murray

Kevin
Mayhew

We hope you enjoy the music in *Recorder Consorts*.
Further copies are available from your local music shop.

In case of difficulty, please contact the publisher direct:

The Sales Department
KEVIN MAYHEW LTD
Rattlesden
Bury St Edmunds
Suffolk IP30 0SZ

Phone 0449 737978
Fax 0449 737834

Please ask for our complete catalogue of outstanding Instrumental Music.

Front Cover: *Dreaming* by Ulpiano Checa Y Sanz (1860-1916).
Reproduced by kind permission of Fine Art Photographic Library, London.

Cover designed by Juliette Clarke and Graham Johnstone.
Picture Research: Jane Rayson.
Music Setting: Tricia Oliver.

First published in Great Britain in 1993 by Kevin Mayhew Ltd.

Contents

ENGLISH	FRANÇAIS	DEUTSCH	ITALIANO
Descant	*Sopran*	*Sopran*	*Sopran*
Treble	*Alto*	*Alt*	*Alto*
Tenor	*Tenor*	*Tenor*	*Tenor*
Bass	*Basse*	*Baß*	*Bass*

DOM GREGORY MURRAY (1905-1992) was best known as an organist and as a composer of church music, but he also enjoyed a high reputation within the world of enthusiastic recorder players. He took up the recorder rather late in life but became a devotee of the instrument, especially favouring the playing of consort music. He made many arrangements for this particular form and the pieces in this collection are evidence of his expertise in this area. He gave much encouragement to recorder groups and for these he would write occasional pieces; *Bach's Delight*, included in this volume, is one of these.

Dom Andrew Moore

MENUET

George Frideric Handel (1685 - 1759)
arranged by Dom Gregory Murray

7

9

MOTET V

Johann Sebastian Bach (1685 - 1750)
arranged by Dom Gregory Murray

13

18

19

PARTITE DIVERSE DI FOLLIA

Bernardo Pasquini (1637 - 1710)
arranged by Dom Gregory Murray

21

22

24

25

26

FANTAZIA

Anthony van Noordt (d. 1675)
arranged by Dom Gregory Murray

29

30

32

33

For the 21st Birthday Party of Bristol Branch S.R.P. 1969

BACH'S DELIGHT

Dom Gregory Murray (1905 - 1992)

39

40

D.S. al Fine

D.S. al Fine

D.S. al Fine

D.S. al Fine

41

PASSAMEZZO PAVAN

Peter Philips (c. 1560 - 1628)
arranged by Dom Gregory Murray

61

PASSACAILLE

George Frideric Handel (1685 - 1759)
arranged by Dom Gregory Murray

65

FOUR DANCES

Melchior Franck (c.1579 - 1639)
arranged by Dom Gregory Murray

72

73

75

LARGHETTO

Johann Joachim Quantz (1697 - 1773)
arranged by Dom Gregory Murray